SPEAKING
TO THE
HEART

SPEAKING TO THE HEART

A Father's Guide to
Growth in Virtue

STEPHEN GABRIEL

Our Sunday Visitor Publishing Division
Our Sunday Visitor, Inc.
Huntington, Indiana 46750

Copyright © 1999 by Stephen Gabriel

ISBN: 0-87973-684-4
LCCCN: 98-67329

Cover design by Tyler Ottinger

PRINTED IN THE UNITED STATES OF AMERICA

*To my wife, Peggy,
and our children, Alex, Claire,
Elena, Kate, Mary, Tom,
Monica, and Suzanne,
who show great patience as I
struggle at living the virtues.*

Speak to his heart, and the man becomes suddenly virtuous.

Ralph Waldo Emerson
Essays, First Series: The Over-Soul

Table of Contents

Introduction

Fathers and Virtues

I wrote this little book as a father for other fathers — specifically for fathers with children in their homes or at least with regular contact with their children. Mothers, grandparents, and single people may enjoy what I have written here and be inspired by it, but these words are primarily aimed at men who are engaged in the day-to-day business of raising their sons and daughters to be godly men and women.

I am sharing some wisdom I have acquired. Some of it has been won the hard way, through the struggles of raising a family, through trial and error, through reflecting on failure and success.

Some of this wisdom has been handed down to me. I am a Catholic, and I draw on the great tradition of what my Church has said about virtue through the centuries. The source of virtue is Christ. The Scriptures teach his way — the way of virtue — and I hope to join you on Christ's path.

Who Am I?

At work I am an expert, by profession an economist for the U.S. government. At home no one thinks I am an expert — especially me. I became a father in 1976. My wife, Peggy, and I now have eight children. I regard my work as a father as the most important thing I do, but like most fathers I have no special training for it. Still I have learned a great deal. My teachers have included my own father, other men I have observed, several close friends, my Church, and a number of wise and holy mentors that I have met through reading. My best teachers have been my wife and children. The wisdom in this book is more along the lines of practical "street smarts" than anything I might have learned by doing a degree in child development, philosophy, or pastoral theology. You can learn much from experts in these fields. Here you will find wisdom of a different sort — lessons from the heart.

Who am I? I'm a man who takes his role as father very seriously. My chief goal is to help my children grow up to be mature, well-adjusted Catholic men and women who take their faith very seriously. I want to help them get to heaven. I'm a man like you.

Why Virtue?

How do we help our children reach that mature faith which will help them to navigate the turbulent currents of life? The answer has a lot to do with virtue. One dictionary I looked at defines virtue as "moral excellence and righteousness; goodness." That's a fairly good working definition of what I am getting at in this little book. It seems to me that our children's success in life, in both human and supernatural terms, will depend on the extent to which they have acquired the virtues.

In this book I look at twenty character traits that I think are important to the lives of a father and his children. They are loosely based on the classic virtues of Catholic tradition. They include the theological virtues of faith, hope, and charity — so-called because they are integral to establishing an intimate relationship with almighty God. They also include the cardinal virtues of prudence, justice, fortitude, and temperance. These are cardinal virtues because they are the fundamental human virtues that must be acquired to reach any level of human perfection. All the other human virtues flow from these. Other human virtues that our children need include humility, poverty, chastity, and industriousness, just to name a few.

Our children will grow in the virtues by repeated acts that require virtue and, of course, by praying for the grace to acquire the virtues they need so much in life. Our example as virtuous men, as men who struggle to live virtuous lives, is crucial to our children's success in ultimately becoming virtuous men and women. We can preach to them about virtues until we are blue in the face. But until they see their fathers struggling (and they will see it as precisely that, a struggle!) to grow in virtue, it will be all talk. Anyone can talk the talk. Talk is, as they say, very cheap! We fathers have to walk the walk — walking, that is, the path of virtue!

Using This Book

Some of what you read here will make you uncomfortable. Pay attention to that. Your discomfort is a piece of wisdom. The problems of fathering are not so much the difficulties we face, but the way we handle the difficulties we face. Over the years my biggest obstacle in fathering has been my own lack of virtue. It has done me no harm to realize that my efforts to live the virtues have fallen short. On the contrary, failure makes us more humble and dependent on almighty God. Our prayer and effort help us to grow in virtue and become the example that our children need.

You are not alone! God is with fathers. God has chosen us to raise our children for him and he will give us the grace we need to succeed. Other fathers are with you too. So, as a father who is still very much in the thick of it, I offer this book of reflections on the virtues — reflections from one Catholic father to another. Together, we can approach our responsibilities as fathers with confidence.

Stephen Gabriel

Chapter **One**

...What matters
is faith that
makes its power
felt through love.

Galatians 5:6

Reason is

our soul's

left hand,

Faith her right,

By these we

reach divinity.

John Donne,
To the Countess of Bedford

Faith

Faith for a Christian is belief in the Bible. It is belief in the God who reveals himself in Scripture and in his teaching. Faith is the virtue by which we believe in all that the Church teaches. Although faith is reasonable and reason can defend it, reason cannot prove it.

It is our faith that enables us to establish a personal relationship with Jesus, becoming his followers. Our faith moves us to live our lives in accordance with his teachings.

It is through the eyes of faith that we see Jesus himself at Mass as both priest and victim. It is our faith that tells us the Eucharist is in fact the body, blood, soul, and divinity of Jesus. And it is through faith that we believe it is Jesus himself who absolves us of our sins in the sacrament of confession, merely using the priest as an instrument.

Our faith is a gift from God. Since it is a gratuitous gift that we do not merit, we can never take it for granted. Faith is a gift that may grow or diminish. Indeed, it is a gift that may be lost. We can lose the gift of faith by turning our backs on God. Yet, like the father of the Prodigal Son, who is a symbol of God himself, our Lord is always looking toward the horizon awaiting our return.

God does not impose himself upon us. However, if we are well disposed, searching for the truth with a sincere heart, he will give us this precious gift of faith.

We grow in faith through prayer, asking the Lord to increase our faith as a child asks for more of his or her favorite dessert. Growing more like a child before God will compel him to give us more faith.

I realize that my faith is not just going to church on Sunday, or reading Sacred Scripture, or accepting certain points of doctrine. Rather, my faith is following the person of Jesus Christ and living my life according to his teaching.

I am prepared to suffer ridicule, misunderstanding, and financial burden for the sake of my faith.

I consider the power of faith as illustrated in the Gospels — blind men see; the dead are raised to life; the crippled are healed — and I know that true faith is no less effective today.

I make the instruction of my children in the faith a high priority. I take time to teach them myself.

I continue to receive the sacraments regularly — even when they apparently "do nothing for me." The grace I receive is working on the "inside." This may be especially true when my Communions are dry and when I seem to get little from participating in Mass.

God gave me an intellect to help me grow in faith. I make the effort to increase my knowledge and understanding of my faith through study.

I realize that God did not give me the gift of faith to keep to myself. I am eager to share my faith with my friends while respecting their freedom of conscience as they discern God's will for themselves.

I know that my faith entails bearing the cross throughout my life. If I try to live a Christian life while avoiding the cross, I am no better off than the rich young man who went away sad (see Matthew 19:16-22).

I try to take the life and teachings of Christ to heart, recognizing that his words are directed at me personally. I am prepared to accept all that comes with living the life of a Christian — sacrifice, obedience, pouring myself out for others. And, of course, I also consider my reward — paradise forever!

Chapter Two

HOPE

I am going to prepare a place for
you, and after I have gone and
prepared you a place, I shall return
to take you with me, so that where
I am you may be too.

John 14:3

Hope is itself a

species of happiness,

and, perhaps, the chief

happiness which this

world affords.

Samuel Johnson

Boswell, *Life*

Hope is the virtue by which we rely on the grace of God to grow in holiness during our lifetime, trusting that we will ultimately see him face to face for all eternity in heaven. It is by hope that we persevere during times of trial and hardship. Our hope keeps us faithful when we are shaken by the suffering of a loved one or when we experience an arid time in our relationship with God.

Without hope there is nothing left but spiritual desolation. If we do not rely on God for the grace to grow in holiness, we seek happiness in worldly pleasure and are destined for disappointment.

As husbands and fathers, we carry a substantial burden of responsibility on our shoulders, which God has placed there. Yet, we have every reason to anticipate our ultimate success. God has placed his confidence in us. And he has given us ample resources. His grace is ours for the asking, and through our regular participation in the sacramental life of the Church we will grow in the virtue of hope, confident in God's guiding hand.

A person of hope radiates optimism, cheerfulness, and confidence, knowing that he is a wayfarer in this world on his way to his ultimate home in heaven. And this knowledge has a profound influence on one's outlook on life. The virtue of hope leads us to contemplate, in the midst of this troubled world, that most profound longing which was articulated by the Apostle: "Eye has not seen, nor ear heard, nor has it entered into the heart of man, what good things God has prepared for those who love him" (1 Corinthians 2:9).

I teach my children that God communicates hope to the world through the Gospel. I urge them to get to know Jesus intimately. It is their friendship with Christ that will bring them through the toughest trials of life.

I acknowledge my sinfulness and beg the Lord's forgiveness, confident that he forgives even my most grievous transgressions. This confidence stems from the teaching of Christ and that outward sign of his mercy, the sacrament of confession.

When in the midst of personal struggle, I turn to God for assistance, approaching him as a small child seeks help from his father.

I focus on almighty God's power and goodness and the fact that he has sought me out to spend the rest of eternity with him in heaven.

I would not deny bringing another child into the world because of society's decadent state of affairs. That child whose existence I deny may just be the instrument that God would use to save many souls.

I pray, with hope, for the conversion of society to a true life of faith. My prayer is accompanied by an apostolic zeal that will help to convert my little corner of the world. That is, I will take concrete steps toward bringing my family and friends closer to God.

When I am tempted to despair, I consider the results of the prayer of the Good Thief: "Remember me when you come into your kingdom" (Luke 23:42). No poor soul is beyond the efficacy of Christ's cross!

In spite of the considerable evil that I see in the world, I look to the future with optimism and confidence, knowing that Jesus did not teach us the Lord's Prayer to frustrate us — "thy kingdom come, thy will be done on Earth...."

When my child strays from the faith, I pray with hope for my lost son or daughter. The lesson of the Prodigal Son is a lesson of hope and love that gives me confidence that my children will receive the grace they need to find their way home again.

Chapter Three

CHARITY

You must love the
Lord your God with all
your heart, with all your
soul, and with all your mind.
This is the greatest and
the first commandment.
The second resembles it:
You must love your neighbor
as yourself.

Matthew 22:37-39

For this

I think charity,

to love God

for himself,

and our neighbor

for God.

Sir Thomas Browne
Religio Medici

Charity

Charity is the virtue by which we love God above all things. And our love for God moves us to love our fellowman. Since God is the source of all love, the capacity of the human heart to love has no limit.

Most importantly, charity is directed at God and manifests itself in our sincere desire and effort to please him — that is, to obey him. The love that we have for God is expressed both internally in our prayer and externally in our actions. In both instances, the proof of our love is our willingness to obey. And for a Christian this frequently means sacrifice. Indeed, our Lord made it clear that obedience and love are inseparable in our relationship with him. "If you love me you will keep my commandments" (John 14:15).

True charity causes us to treat unpleasant people with kindness because they too are children of God. If we have charity, we give of ourselves when it is inconvenient to do so or when the object of our charity is someone we don't particularly like.

As fathers, we live the virtue of charity by correcting a misbehaving child with kindness; or by giving up some of "our personal time" to spend time with our kids or with our wives. We are called to be the servants of the family.

Christ provided us with the ultimate example of love. The life of Christ teaches us that true charity or love is expressed by such things as sacrifice, self-surrender, and service. The Gospels provide us with a comprehensive guide to loving. Our Lord surrendered everything and then beckons us, "Follow me!"

I consider that God makes clear how he wants to be loved. He wants me to be obedient to his commandments. This frequently means doing what he wants, not what I want!

I read Sacred Scripture and make an effort to understand the moral teaching of the Church. I put as much effort into learning about God as I do into learning about secular matters.

I reflect on Paul's description of charity point by point: Charity is patient, kind, not jealous or boastful, not arrogant or rude, does not insist on its own way (see 1 Corinthians 13:4-7). I am especially concerned with how I measure up at home in my relationship with my wife and children.

Considerations for Growth
in the Virtue of **Charity**

I make a list of the people I know who need my prayers, and I glance over the names each day while I pray.

I pray every day, asking God to reveal his will for me. I consult an adviser to help me progress on my path to holiness.

I give of my time (more precious than gold) to some worthy cause and try to involve my kids.

I am mindful of the needs of my wife and I try to go out of my way to lighten her load, even at the expense of my own schedule.

I try to focus on the needs of my family rather than my own. I remind myself that I am the servant of my family, not its lord and master.

Chapter Four

PRUDENCE

Or if it be virtue you love, why,
virtues are the fruit of her labors,
since it is she who teaches
temperance and prudence,
justice and fortitude; nothing in
life is more serviceable to
men than these.

Wisdom 8:7

Wise venturing

is the most commendable

part of human prudence.

**George Savile
(Lord Halifax)**
*Political, Moral, and
Miscellaneous Reflections*

Prudence

Prudence is the foundation of virtuous men. It gives them sound judgment and discernment in difficult situations. Prudence allows one to practice all the virtues with delicacy, discretion, and reason. Prudence enables us to overcome our emotions, assess the facts of the situation within the context of the moral law, and make a wise decision.

Too often we shoot from the hip, taking the path of least resistance when faced with a controversial decision regarding the family. A prudent father considers his ultimate objective — the eternal happiness of each member of the family — when making important decisions.

The practice of this virtue touches every aspect of our lives. Consequently, we have many occasions to practice it. We are prudent when we do what is morally right in spite of any potential adverse consequences. We are also prudent when we choose a morally neutral course of action to avoid an adverse outcome. We grow in prudence if we have a well-formed conscience and learn from our mistakes.

We must pray especially to the Holy Spirit to give us light and increase in us the virtue of prudence. As fathers, we are faced with many decisions that demand prudent consideration — changing jobs, deciding whether our teenager should attend a particular event, choosing the right school for our children.

Humility also plays a role here. We fathers need to know when the prudent thing to do is to simply listen to our wives.

I always pray to God for guidance before making an important decision.

I consult reliable film reviews for the moral content of movies prior to seeing them and certainly before allowing my children to see them.

Before taking a new job, I consider the potential impact on my family in terms of how the job will influence my availability to them.

I seek advice from experts that I can trust in areas such as family finances.

I take a hands-on approach to shaping the tone of my home. My wife and I agree on how we manage television viewing of our family — ourselves included.

We seek advice and discuss how to handle teaching our children about their sexuality. We also consider how and when our children date. We are timely in addressing these issues, keeping in mind that our children will grow up faster than we like to think.

I am not swayed by popular opinion or practice. I am prepared to swim against the current of popular thinking in moral matters and teach my children to do the same.

When I consider my children's education I recognize that what they need is an education for life. They must acquire certain knowledge. But, most importantly, they must learn how to think, discern, and act like Christian men and women.

Chapter **Five**

JUSTICE

You must not be guilty of unjust
verdicts. You must neither be partial
to the little man nor overawed by
the great; you must pass judgment
on your neighbor according
to justice.

Leviticus 19:15

All knowledge

that is divorced from justice

must be called cunning

rather than wisdom.

Plato
Cicero, *De Officiis*

Justice

Justice is the virtue that enables one to give to each person his due. This assumes that we all have certain rights that we expect to be honored. These rights include such things as a right to life, freedom, private property, and the dignity and respect owed to all human beings. We have a right to our good name and a right to educate our children as we see fit.

Unfortunately, the sins against justice are many. We sin against justice when we rob people of their good name through gossip; when we fail to pay our debts; when we neglect to worship God as he desires.

As husbands and fathers, we are called to respect the rights of each member of our family. It is particularly easy for us to forget that our children have certain rights that must be protected. Each member of the family has the right to pursue his own interests and hobbies provided they are not inconsistent with the overall good and well-being of the family. And each family member has the right to worship God in the manner that his conscience leads him.

All people have the right to live under conditions that are consistent with basic human dignity — having access to adequate food, shelter, clothing, education, and medical care. As Christians, we cannot ignore this fundamental need.

Through prayer, a knowledge of the moral law, and daily examination of conscience, we can grow in justice, a virtue so important and fundamental that St. Joseph was described by St. Matthew simply as being a just man.

I recognize that the natural law, as articulated in the Ten Commandments, presents a serious admonition from God himself to live the virtue of justice in all aspects of my life.

I worship God and respect his name out of love. But, out of justice, I continue to worship, even when the emotions of love are missing.

I work hard, giving my employer a day's work for a day's wage.

I make every effort to pay my debts, even when it involves great sacrifice.

I treat my wife with love and respect and with a lifelong commitment to fidelity. I do this freely out of love, even though I know that I am obliged to do this out of justice.

I don't gossip. And I avoid the sin of detraction — that is, unnecessarily saying something that is true about someone that damages his reputation.

I work as hard as necessary to provide for my family, keeping in mind that my children do not have a right to go to Harvard or Yale. They do have a right to have their father actively engaged in their upbringing.

I exercise my civic duties to protect the legitimate rights of others, especially those who may not be in a strong position to defend their own rights.

I consider the fact that, although God is all loving, he is also all just and he won't coerce me to choose to be with him forever in heaven.

Chapter Six

FORTITUDE

In the world you will have trouble,

but be brave: I have conquered

the world.

John 16:33

Where true fortitude dwells,

loyalty, bounty, friendship,

and fidelity may be found.

Sir Thomas Browne
Christian Morals

Fortitude

Fortitude is the toughness to do what we know we must do in spite of difficulties. The dictionary proposes the following synonyms: grit, backbone, pluck, guts, sand. It sounds like a description of a middle linebacker. Yet, living a truly Christian life is a much tougher job. And the stakes are much higher. For example, if we fail in our role as fathers, we stand to lose much more than the national championship. We stand to lose our very soul and possibly the souls of the children that God has given us to raise for him.

When we act in prudence and in justice we can exercise the virtue of fortitude with confidence. As fathers, we need a confident and calm fortitude to preserve a truly Christian culture in our family.

In a perfect world, fortitude might not be as decisive a virtue for fathers to practice. In today's world, we must beg our Lord for more and more fortitude to ensure that we don't compromise the principles that we stand for.

*I take my family to church on Sundays,
even when it is inconvenient to do so.*

*I pray and read from the Scriptures each
day in spite of the fact that, at times, I really
don't feel like it.*

*I don't use TV as a baby-sitter when I need
a break from a disagreeable child.*

*I don't submit to peer pressure in
structuring my lifestyle. I have established
Christ as my model, not Pierre Cardin.*

*I resist the temptation to be mesmerized by
television when I am bored. I find
something else to do unless I know of a
program truly worth watching.*

I am prepared to make the financial sacrifices necessary to provide my children with the kind of education they need.

I am firm in my commitment to make our home a truly Christian environment for my family.

I make sure that the clothing worn by my children is modest. The standard that I use is basic Christian modesty — not the standard of popular style. I am convinced that the battle is worth fighting. And it is fought with both firmness and affection.

I don't give in to pressure from my kids when they want to do something that they shouldn't. I try to explain my reasoning when appropriate.

Chapter Seven

TEMPERANCE

All the fighters at the games go into
strict training; they do this just to
win a wreath that will wither away,
but we do it for a wreath that will
never wither. That is how I run,
intent on winning; that is how I fight,
not beating the air. I treat my body
hard and make it obey me, for,
having been an announcer myself,
I should not want to be disqualified.

1 Corinthians 9:25-27

Temperance is

a bridle of gold.

Robert Burton
Anatomy of Melancholy

Temperance

Temperance is evidenced by a sense of moderation and restraint in the exercise of our appetites. However, the practice of the virtue of temperance is much more than simply not being intemperate — that is, overeating, overdrinking, or being unchaste.

Our temperance, motivated by the love of God, must enable our appetites to fulfill their God-given purposes. Indeed, a lack of temperance is a disorder and suggests a certain slavery to our senses. And Christ made it clear that we can have but one master.

Without this supernatural motive, the practice of temperance may seem absurd. If one is good, two must be better. The 1970s motto "If it feels good, do it!" is certainly operative today. This is because of our fallen nature, which makes living the virtue of temperance an ongoing struggle. And the problem is exacerbated by the consumer society in which we live.

Temperance provides us with a certain balance. As human beings, we consist of both body and spirit. In a certain sense, our temperance prevents our body from dominating our spirit and enables us to establish a friendship with God.

I reflect on how I seek my happiness and fulfillment. Do I pursue the acquisition of things and sensual pleasure? Or, do I find my happiness in the service of others and my relationship with God, my Father?

At meals, I take just a little less than what I'd like of one dish.

I try to emphasize the social aspect of meals with family and friends. I am more attentive to the people I am with than to the food and drink. I try to make family meals a time of pleasant conversation.

When I drink alcoholic beverages, I do so to be sociable. I am careful not to drink too much — what a scandal for a Christian!

I don't engage in conversation about food as if it were the focal point of my life. That is, I try to avoid gushing about a meal.

I try not to snack at the slightest provocation. However, I might schedule a snack for a particular time of day.

Considerations for Growth
in the Virtue of **Temperance**

I am sensitive to the desires of my wife at bedtime and try to be affectionate in the way she wants me to be affectionate.

When reading the newspaper and magazines and when watching television, I try to guard my eyes from looking at material that may compromise my values as a Christian.

When I am angry with someone, I try not to "fly off the handle." I wait to calm down and address the issue later.

I use restraint when purchasing a car, computer, or other major items, taking care that I don't pay for more bells and whistles than I really need.

When I am thirsty, I get a drink of water, but wait a few moments before I take a drink. A small thing, true, but doesn't sanctity come from a lifetime of such small things?

Chapter **Eight**

HUMILITY

Anyone who exalts himself will
be humbled, and anyone who
humbles himself will be exalted.

Matthew 23:12

Humble because

of knowledge,

mighty by sacrifice.

Rudyard Kipling
The Islanders

Humility

Humility is the virtue that allows us to see ourselves as we are. It does not deny our gifts and talents; rather, it recognizes that all of our talents and possessions are given to us by God. Humility allows us to establish a proper relationship with God — a relationship that acknowledges our weakness and his power. It is a relationship of dependence.

Pride, on the other hand, tends to put us on a pedestal. It inflates our self-importance. Pride makes us slow to forgive and easily wounded when we are criticized or misunderstood. And our pride makes it so difficult to admit our mistakes and grow in self-knowledge.

It is difficult to be humble in a society that idolizes personal independence to the extent that ours does. Dependence on anyone or anything is generally considered a sign of weakness. Yet, a man of wisdom understands that humility is based on a fundamental truth. Indeed, humility embraces the truth that, as you said, Lord, without you I can do nothing.

I am quick to pray to God for help in all aspects of my life, recognizing that this poor creature needs his help in everything.

I see that I have many shortcomings that blur my vision as a father. I have to struggle daily to overcome them, begging for God's grace and assistance.

I accept the fact that I make mistakes regularly. And I am not too proud to apologize to my family.

I recognize my talents and strengths as gifts from God and know that I will be held accountable at the end of my life for how I used these gifts.

I don't make myself the center of attention. I take an active interest in the concerns of my family, friends, and colleagues.

I thank the Lord for all his blessings, especially for those countless blessings bestowed on me without my knowledge.

*I examine my conscience each day and try
to uncover those faults that keep me from
growing closer to God and my family,
praying, as I do so, the plea of the blind
Bartimaeus, "Rabboni, that I may see" (see
Mark 10:46-52).*

*I am thankful for the incredible talents and
abilities that I see in others. What a
backward world it would be if society had
to rely only on my brainpower.*

*I recognize that, although I know I can have
a profound influence on the lives of my
children, God has made them free to
accept him or reject him.*

*I approach God on my knees with a simple
request: Give my children the grace to
become the disciples you want them to be.*

Chapter Nine

POVERTY

How happy are the poor in spirit;

theirs is the kingdom of heaven.

Matthew 5:3

It is not the man who has

too little, but the man who

craves more, that is poor.

Seneca
Epistulae ad Lucilium

Poverty

Jesus calls all Christians to be poor in spirit. Hence, the poverty that we must aspire to is an interior detachment from worldly possessions. Poverty does not mean living without possessions, but rather having and using them in a way that serves God, our families, and our neighbor.

It might be worthwhile to picture ourselves in our casket a month or so after our death — not a pretty sight! Our possessions will not spare us this destiny. Nor will they make us happy in this life. It seems the more we have, the more difficult it is to focus on the things that will truly last.

Through our competence and hard work we can seek to earn as much income as possible, provided we do not shortchange our responsibilities to our family. We are stewards of the means at our disposal. Through our spirit of poverty, we are prepared to give up our possessions, if that is God's will. Our happiness is not based on our material possessions, but on our relationship with God and others.

I take good care of my things so that they last.

I am generous with my money. That is, I give just a little more than what is comfortable.

When I pay my bills, the first checks are for those alms that I have committed to give.

I evaluate regularly whether I spend enough time with my family. Is my work taking over my life? I discuss this with a friend who gives me his candid opinion.

I maintain my serenity when my paycheck evaporates before the pile of bills stacked up in front of me.

I place my financial difficulties squarely in the hands of God while doing everything humanly possible to alleviate these problems.

I don't collect "toys" I don't really need.

I avoid extravagance and ostentation in the way I live while maintaining a lifestyle appropriate to my station in life.

I don't allow myself to be impressed by wealth. And I teach my children this lesson as well. Rather, I remind myself and my family that a person's worth is not measured by his possessions but by every drop of the blood of Christ. That is, Christ died for all men — the rich and the poor; the educated and the ignorant. We are all valuable in the eyes of God!

I regard my children as gifts from God, not a financial burden. As valuable gifts, they require special care and attention. Even as we struggle to raise them properly, we experience great joy — the joy of cooperating with God in helping to prepare those souls for heaven!

Chapter Ten

CHASTITY

But I say this to you: if a man looks
at a woman lustfully, he has already
committed adultery with her in
his heart.

Matthew 5:28

Chastity enables the soul

to breathe a pure air in the

foulest places.

Joubert
Pensées No. 78

Chastity

Chastity in marriage is a virtue driven by love and respect — love for God and our wives and respect for God's design for our sexuality. Chastity in marriage calls for self-control. Call it self-mastery. Our sexuality must be oriented to the beloved. Indeed, the pleasure that is derived is only good when it comes from a mutual self-giving. We must struggle to live chastely in our marriage because we are weak; we are selfish; and we are influenced powerfully by the world and its values, which are so effectively promulgated by the media.

Chastity in marriage is a universally misunderstood concept. It is widely held that once we reach adulthood and marriage, anything goes in the realm of sex. This seems to apply to entertainment as well as our sexual relations with our wives. The struggle to live chastely within marriage is not unlike the struggle in which unmarried people must engage. Under both circumstances restraint and self-control are required. Both demand a prudent guarding of our senses and a respect and understanding of our sexual instincts. Consequently, a single man who has struggled to be chaste is far better prepared for living chastely in marriage.

Chastity is a difficult virtue for many men to live. But it is not impossible! If we are prepared to struggle and pray and rely on the intercession of our Blessed Mother, God will give us the grace to persevere and emerge victorious.

I reflect on the profound meaning of human sexuality — a man and a woman committed for life to cooperate with God to bring life into the world and prepare that life to live in a manner pleasing to the Creator. And the vehicle of this cooperation is an unselfish love given to each other without holding anything back. This is pure love!

I make sure that the media that enter my home (TV, videos, books, and magazines) characterize human sexuality in a way consistent with God's design.

My conversation reflects the dignity of a child of God. I avoid off-color "jokes" that offend the sensibilities of a Christian.

I am prudent in my dealings with other women, whether in a work or social setting. I must be convinced that I am capable of the most grievous infidelity.

Considerations for Growth
in the Virtue of **Chastity**

I ask God for the grace to conquer my passions.

I guard my eyes and my imagination, especially when I come across women who are dressed immodestly or provocatively. I see, but I don't look!

When reading the newspaper or otherwise acceptable magazines, I pass over articles that might feed my imagination inappropriately. I want an intimate relationship with only one woman, and I married her.

I find other ways to express my affection for my wife during those times when we wish to exercise abstinence.

I am prepared to struggle to grow in the virtue of chastity for the rest of my life. I try to have a sporting spirit in this regard while recognizing its importance. The key is: "Don't get discouraged and don't give up."

Chapter Eleven

INTEGRITY

Honest men have their own
honesty for guidance,
treacherous men are ruined
by their own perfidy.

Proverbs 11:3

I hope I shall always
possess firmness and
virtue enough to maintain
what I consider the most
enviable of all titles, the
character of an
"Honest Man."

George Washington
Moral Maxims

Integrity

Integrity is the consistency between what we know to be real and true and what we communicate about that reality. We lie when we know that what we say is different from reality. Lying is a misuse of the gift of speech that was given to us by God to communicate the truth.

Integrity is also the consistency between our principles of life or belief and the way we live our lives. When we fail to live as our principles dictate, we are simply hypocrites. Of course, it is not hypocritical to periodically fail to live according to our Christian principles because of weakness. But for a professed Christian to live a life without struggling to grow in all the virtues while claiming to embrace the Christian faith is to live a lie.

Integrity spawns trust. And there is nothing more damaging to a relationship than the loss of trust. Without trust we can be little more than acquaintances.

Unfortunately, we tend to pick and choose those situations that call for integrity. We can lie to the IRS about our taxable income. Or we can tell lies to our employer about why we can't get in to work today. And we might wear a cross around our necks proclaiming our belief in Christ's doctrine of the cross while making comfort the priority of our lives. These lies and inconsistencies are obstacles to our growth in integrity. They do us great harm.

As Christians, we must have a passion for the truth. We grow in integrity when we communicate the truth in matters that cost us and under circumstances where we will likely not be caught.

My loyalty to the truth exceeds any authority that I might encounter in this world. No employer or government authority can coerce me to embrace what is false for their sake or for my advancement.

I am honest when I pay my taxes each year. I may use every legal loophole available. But my tax return presents a true statement of my legal obligation to the government.

I don't make excuses for myself when I fail to perform. I accept responsibility for my performance and my behavior.

I regard the confidence placed in me as something absolutely sacred. I must never violate that confidence.

I am true to my beliefs. And I pray for the grace to stand up for the truth, even in the face of severe hardship.

When I notice that a cashier gives me too much change or when I am undercharged on a bill, I correct the error as promptly as possible.

I am willing to risk losing a friend for the sake of the truth. What kind of friend would lie to a friend so as not to rock the boat? This is particularly vital if I must tell my friend that he offends God in some matter!

I am not a "yes man" with superiors at work. If someone asks for my opinion, I use tact and diplomacy as needed and tell him the truth as I see it.

Chapter **Twelve**

PATIENCE

My brothers, you will always have
your trials but, when they come, try
to treat them as a happy privilege;
you understand that your faith is only
put to the test to make you patient,
but patience too is to have its
practical results so that you will
become fully-developed, complete,
with nothing missing.

James 1:2-4

We shall sooner
have the fowl by
hatching the egg
than by smashing it.

Abraham Lincoln
Speech, April 11, 1865

Patience

Patience allows us to bear difficult circumstances calmly. Although we have differing degrees of patience, we all are tested regularly. We must be patient with our children, wives, and others, as well as ourselves.

Parenting is probably the toughest and certainly the most important job we have. And most of us rely on "on-the-job" training as we learn this role. Being patient with ourselves as we learn from our mistakes keeps us from becoming frustrated and discouraged.

Exercising patience out of love when it is difficult to do so is the way that parents substitute for Simon of Cyrene, who assisted Christ on the road to Calvary. How good God is for giving us so many opportunities!

It is our confidence in God's grace that enables us to grow in patience. As we grow in faith and hope, we acquire an inner peace that yields greater patience because we see life from a different perspective. That is, we have a more supernatural outlook.

As with other virtues, we grow in patience through practice and prayer. It is worthwhile to consider just how patient our Lord is with us day in and day out — year in and year out — when we brood over the demands on our patience.

Considerations for Growth
in the Virtue of **Patience**

*When my child makes me angry I try to
cool off before addressing the issue, if
possible.*

*When I reprimand my child I make it clear
that I dislike the behavior — not rny child.*

*When I drive my car I try to behave as if my
pastor were sitting in the passenger seat. I
don't like the impatient personality that
emerges when I become the anonymous
driver.*

*I try to remember that God's pace is
usually not my pace. If things happened as
fast as I wanted, I might never drop to my
knees and beg for God's help.*

*I pray to God daily for an increase in
patience.*

*I go out of my way to be affectionate with
the child that I find most trying at this time.*

I try to keep quiet and accept the fact that my wife and I approach certain tasks differently. My way is not necessarily the only way. It may not even be the right way!

When I help my children with their homework, I try to put other things out of my mind and focus myself on my child's needs.

I try to remind myself that the effort I make to give the patient smile that I don't feel like giving may be just the cross that Jesus has asked me to bear today.

I am patient with my children as I wait anxiously for them to emerge from the difficult stage they are now going through.

Chapter **Thirteen**

CHEERFULNESS

God loves a cheerful giver.

2 Corinthians 9:7

The most manifest sign

of wisdom is a continual

cheerfulness.

Montaigne
Essays

Cheerfulness

Cheerfulness comes to all Christians convinced that they are children of God. Cheerfulness is born out of our relationship with Christ. Hence, its origins are supernatural. This is why people who are undergoing severe hardship can be very cheerful and tend to inspire those of us who complain about relatively small problems.

People who suffer can be cheerful because they see their hardships as the cross of Christ — the cross that they were called to bear. Hence, human suffering has a profound meaning to the Christian. It has a redemptive value that, when properly understood, brings joy to the heart of those who endure it.

That is not to say that suffering is easy. If it were easy, it wouldn't be suffering. But, with the grace of God and faith in the Gospel of our Lord, difficulties and hardship can be endured cheerfully.

Even when things are going well, we may need to remind ourselves to brighten our demeanor. This can be done by focusing our attention less on ourselves and more on others. Our life of prayer and frequent reflection on our many blessings will help us to keep our lives in perspective in good times and in bad.

Most of us have to deal with small inconveniences and contradictions daily. And it is easy to let these little pinpricks influence our demeanor. However, by struggling — sometimes heroically — to overcome our inclination to allow these unpleasant matters to darken our days, we proclaim our faith in Jesus as eloquently as the most polished orator.

Considerations for Growth
in the Virtue of **Cheerfulness**

*I try to keep in mind that Christian
cheerfulness is not a silly grin that is only
skin-deep. It is an attitude that reflects the
state of my soul.*

*I make an effort to greet my family, friends,
and colleagues with a smile, even when I
don't feel like it.*

*I don't bring my problems from work home
with me in the evening. That is, I don't
allow them to affect my mood.*

*I give each member of my family the
attention he or she wants and needs when
I get home from work, inquiring, "How was
your day?"*

*When I am inconvenienced or delayed, I try
to see the situation as an opportunity to
rise above my strictly human inclinations
and take a more supernatural outlook by
offering this little cross for my wife and kids.*

*I don't hold grudges or dwell on injustices
that may have been done to me.*

*When I am tempted to feel sorry for myself,
I reflect on the blessings that have been
bestowed on me — starting with the gift of
faith — and ask our Lord for the grace to
overcome these feelings.*

*When I find that I lack cheerfulness, I
examine my conscience to determine the
cause. I remind myself that my sullen mood
is inconsistent with living the virtue of hope.
I am destined for heaven!*

*When things are not going as well as I like,
I remind myself that this can be the cross
of Christ, if I allow it to be. What a different
perspective I have when I see myself as a
co-redeemer!*

*I try to remember that a perfect remedy for
sadness is prayer. Another good remedy is
to help someone in need.*

Chapter Fourteen

INDUSTRIOUSNESS

We gave you a rule when we were
with you: not to let anyone have any
food if he refused to do any work.

2 Thessalonians 3:10

Originality and the feeling

of one's own dignity are

achieved only through work

and struggle.

Dostoyevsky
The Diary of a Writer

Industriousness

Industriousness is a virtue that is characterized by hard work and work well done. This work is an activity carried out by man in cooperation with the ongoing creative action of God. That is, God created man to work. Work is not a punishment imposed on us as a result of the fall of Adam. Indeed, prior to the fall, "Yahweh God took the man [Adam] and settled him in the garden of Eden to cultivate and take care of it" (Genesis 2:15). The work of the industrious man glorifies God when it is performed well and when it is done for motives that are pleasing to almighty God.

God intended all people to work. Anything else would be beneath our dignity as children of God. This is why unemployment is such a demoralizing and demeaning situation. We all need to work.

Most men spend the better part of a day at their work. Clearly, this time is not intended to be some sort of spiritual wasteland where we never lift our hearts to God. For us Christians, our time of work must also be a time of prayer. And we can accomplish this by offering our work to God each day and renewing that offering during the day. Since this offering is to our God, we try to offer him the most perfect gift we can — our work well done to the best of our abilities.

Considerations for Growth
in the Virtue of **Industriousness**

I see my work as a way of using the gifts and talents given to me by God for his greater glory and the service of others.

At the beginning of the day, I offer my work to God and ask him to bless it.

I try to work as effectively as possible, not wasting time.

I try to persevere at the difficult or disagreeable tasks without complaining or making the lives of others unpleasant.

In my work around the house, I try to involve my children, teaching them the value of a job well done.

I make the effort to maintain and improve my skills so that I can grow in my capabilities and effectiveness.

I establish little spiritual oases that can help me to maintain a sense of the presence of God at my place of work. For example, I might make it a habit of saying a brief prayer when I enter the elevator or when the phone rings.

I recognize that my efforts to be punctual, organized, and disciplined at work allow me to get more work done in a shorter period of time, giving me more time for my family.

When I examine my conscience each day, I consider how I use my time at work and how I can improve my work, making it a more perfect offering to God.

Chapter **Fifteen**

FRIENDSHIP

I shall not call you servants any
more, because a servant does not
know his master's business; I call
you friends, because I have made
known to you everything I have
learned from my Father.

John 15:15

Friendship is a

union of spirits,

a marriage of hearts,

and the bond thereof virtue.

William Penn
adapted from
Some Fruits of Solitude

Friendship

True friendship comes from a knowledge of the befriended — a knowledge of the inner person. In other words, what makes him "tick." And this knowledge is acquired when two individuals share what is important to them. They share their aspirations, their hopes, and their fears. They become vulnerable to some extent.

In our society today, friendships are difficult to make because we have become rather impersonal. We are very busy. We are busy with our work, our families, and our hobbies. And it is impossible to develop a friendship if we don't take the time to get to know someone.

Yet, friendships can be a wonderful support for families. Friends can provide moral support in our struggle to live a truly Christian life, faithful to the Gospel.

Let's face it, if enough people question our goals and objectives, sooner or later we start to question them as well and abandon the values that we try so hard to incorporate into our lives and the lives of our children. If we have many friends with the same values and aspirations, we can get the support we need during the tough times.

Of course, we can have great friendships with individuals of other faiths. And, as disciples of Christ, we can and should utilize our friendship to bring these friends closer to God. What a wonderful display of friendship!

I go out of my way to get together with my friends so that we can maintain and deepen our friendship.

I try to be sensitive to the concerns of my friends and whether they need help of any kind.

When a friend needs a correction, I tell him what he needs to hear with affection, tact, and firmness if called for.

I thank my friend for giving me the correction that I need, knowing that it was probably more painful for him to give me the correction than it was for me to receive it.

When a friend moves away, I try to keep in touch through letters, electronic mail, and occasionally the telephone.

I recognize that my best friend is my wife. I try not to take our friendship for granted, but make the effort to deepen our friendship through regular communication. I am prepared to work at this.

I remind myself that friendliness can foster friendships with people I otherwise would not get to know. And as an apostle, I really should make an effort to expand my circle of friends.

When I ride on public transportation, I strike up a conversation with the person sitting next to me rather than keep my nose buried in a book or newspaper.

I get involved at my kids' school and try to get to know the parents of their classmates.

I make an effort to get to know the people at work, my kids' school friends and teachers, and others that I encounter each day. I try to be friendly and show an interest in them.

Chapter Sixteen

LOYALTY

Near the cross of Jesus stood his
mother and his mother's sister,
Mary the wife of Clopas, and Mary
of Magdala. Seeing his mother and
the disciple he loved standing near
her, Jesus said to his mother,
"Woman, this is your son." Then to
the disciple he said, "This is your
mother." And from that moment the
disciple made a place for her
in his home.

John 19:25-27

It is better to be

faithful than famous.

Theodore Roosevelt
Riis, *Theodore Roosevelt, The Citizen*

Loyalty

Loyalty is one of the more character-defining virtues. It is a virtue that emerges when the going gets tough. One does not sing the praises of a patriot who is loyal to his country in the midst of peace and prosperity. Loyalty is demonstrated by a willingness to put one's life, reputation, or well-being on the line for a cause that is greater than oneself.

We begin to acquire the virtue of loyalty as children when we learn to be loyal to our friends and family. However, these lessons come hard for children. And it is usually our parents who teach us the importance of loyalty in these relationships. Our sense of loyalty grows as we mature and find opportunities to practice the virtue in various situations.

In marriage we make a promise before God and society to be faithful to our wives under all circumstances for the rest of our lives. We are faithful in spite of temptations, marital difficulties, financial problems, or poor health.

At one time or another every marriage is challenged to some degree. At these times our commitment to fidelity, along with the grace of God, pulls us through and enables us to build an even stronger marriage.

I look for occasions to teach my children the importance of loyalty among family and friends. I explain that sometimes it takes great bravery to stand up for a brother, sister, or friend who is not being treated fairly.

I am quick to defend the Church when attacked or unjustifiably criticized.

I show my loyalty to my country by voting and helping to find solutions to its problems rather than simply complaining.

When a friend is having a difficult time, I try to help even if, at the time, my help is not wanted.

When a friend is the subject of gossip, I defend him and do my best to restore his good name.

I renew my wedding vows privately, in my prayers, asking our Lord for the grace to be faithful always.

I am discreet in conversations regarding my supervisors. It is so easy to criticize when someone else has to make the decisions.

I consider that every sin I commit is a betrayal of Christ crucified. I try to remember that he saw me and loved me as he hung from the cross on Calvary. This kind of love demands loyalty.

I struggle to be faithful in the little things, remembering the great reward promised for such fidelity. "Well done, good and faithful servant; you have shown you can be faithful in small things, I will trust you with greater; come and join in your master's happiness" (Matthew 25:21).

Chapter Seventeen

PERSEVERANCE

Be as confident now, then, since
the reward is so great. You will need
endurance to do God's will and
gain what he has promised.

Hebrews 10:35-36

Endure and persist;

this pain will turn to

your good by and by.

Ovid
Amores

Perseverance

Perseverance is the virtue that helps us to maintain a course of action, purpose, or belief. It allows us to stay on the right track in spite of difficulties and setbacks.

Perseverance is required of anyone who pursues a challenging goal. It takes no perseverance to be swept along by the tide of life, doing what comes easy. However, a demanding course of studies or a long period of athletic training to prepare for a major event requires a high level of perseverance.

As Christian husbands and fathers, we find that perseverance is paramount to our success. So often we find ourselves going against the grain. Indeed, a Christian's values are always under attack. And because we are weak, there is always the risk that we will compromise those values.

Even under the best of circumstances, building a solid Christian family requires perseverance. In spite of our many faults and weaknesses, we must endeavor to instill virtues in our children as they grow and mature. And each child will bring his or her own set of challenges. Of course, building a strong and happy marriage requires a good deal of effort as well. In spite of the love we have for our wives, the nitty-gritty of two individuals sharing a life together brings conflicts and disagreements that must be worked out so that the family can live in a spirit of love and harmony.

We must pray to God for perseverance each day so that we can continue the good fight. And we can be confident of our success in spite of our own shortcomings.

Raising children in today's world is difficult in many respects. I try to stay focused on my objective while facing the day-to-day challenge of instilling Christian virtues in my children.

I recognize that I have many faults and weaknesses. I am prepared to struggle daily to overcome them.

My faith will be challenged by the "conventional wisdom" and by my own tendency to lukewarmness. I meet this challenge by daily study and prayer and trust in God's mercy and grace.

Consumerism is like a temptress who will not give up until she has lured the wavering man into her arms. I struggle to persevere in my spirit of poverty and my willingness to sacrifice to remain faithful to my Christian calling. Attachment to things necessarily keeps me from deepening my friendship with Christ.

*The lax mores of our society will seduce
our children without our vigilance and
guidance. The risk is that we give up, worn
down by the struggle. However, our
consistent message to our children will
help them to understand, in time, the
wisdom of that message.*

*I recognize that my marriage vows are for
life. I persevere in addressing any problems
that might threaten my marriage.*

*I do not allow TV to corrupt the tone of my
home. Television is used sparingly by my
family. I am consistent in enforcing this
policy in spite of any pressures exerted by
my children.*

*I persevere in my prayer remembering that
Jesus taught us to "pray continually and
never lose heart" (Luke 18:1).*

*I try to put the difficulties of life into
perspective — years of struggle versus an
eternity of happiness.*

Chapter Eighteen

COURAGE

And now take courage

and be men of valor.

2 Samuel 2:7

Life only demands from you

the strength you possess.

Only one feat is possible

— not to have run away.

Dag Hammarskjöld
Markings

Courage

Courage is a word that evokes images of combat, warfare, and danger. Indeed, courage is demonstrated whenever we do what is right in spite of an imminent or potential threat. The threat that we fathers face usually does not put our lives in danger. Rather, we are threatened with misunderstanding, ridicule, financial hardship, and failure.

It is not unusual to face situations in the workplace that demand courage. It can take courage to tell the boss that we have to leave work on time in order to be home for dinner. It would take great courage to change jobs or even careers so that our job is more compatible with family life.

Courage is frequently needed when making tough family decisions. These situations can arise when deciding on where to send our children to school, or if a child needs to stop seeing a friend who is a bad influence.

Our society presents Christian fathers with many reasons for courage. We are labeled intolerant because we take our faith seriously and fight for our rights as parents. We are ridiculed because the size of our family is larger than the national average.

Courage and daring are needed to bring children into the world and teach them to swim against the tide. Yet, if we are convinced that we are doing God's work and utilize the grace that he makes available, we can be confident of our ultimate success.

I bring children into this troubled world with confidence in God's providence. He is the source of my courage. By relying on him, my victory is ensured.

I pattern my life after the teachings of Christ, knowing that many look at me and my way of life with contempt.

I am not ashamed to speak the truth, even if I hold a minority opinion.

I adhere to my principles in the face of hardship or misunderstanding, demonstrating an everyday courage that strengthens my family.

I carry out an active apostolate, trying to bring my friends and colleagues closer to God. I persevere with courage, knowing that many turn their backs on the grace being offered to them.

I face illness and medical problems with courage and confidence in God's will. I try to be cheerful and use these circumstances to grow closer to our Lord.

I initiate ambitious projects without fear of failing. I act with prudence and good judgment and I seek advice. But I proceed with a degree of daring, knowing that failing is not always failure but acquired experience.

I consider that death is not the end of life but the passage to eternity. Fear of death is only for those at enmity with Christ. Death, for a friend of Jesus, can then be more easily accepted as the will of God.

I participate in the political process with courage, doing everything I can to change unjust laws — those that violate the natural law.

Chapter Nineteen

GENEROSITY

Tell them that they are to do good,
and be rich in good works, to be
generous and willing to share — this
is the way they can save up a good
capital sum for the future if they
want to make sure of the only life
that is real.

1 Timothy 6:18-19

Generosity is the

flower of justice.

Hawthorne
American Note-Books

Generosity

Generosity is the virtue that exposes the heart of a person. It is the fruit of true Christian love. As disciples of Christ, we are called to imitate him in all things. And the central feature of the life of our Lord was his generosity. He came into the world to give. Indeed, he gave everything he had — even his very life.

A generous soul is detached from his possessions — especially his most precious possession, his time. As fathers, we must rid ourselves of any notion that our time is our own. At work our time belongs to our employer. And at home it is for our family.

Clearly, God expects our generosity to extend beyond our family. Our generosity to others is a natural outgrowth of our love of God and a reflection of our understanding that we are mere stewards of the gifts and talents given to us by our Creator.

Indeed, Jesus so identifies with the weak and vulnerable that our negligence in meeting their needs is really a neglect of our Lord's needs. "Next he will say to those on his left hand, 'Go away from me, with your curse upon you, to the eternal fire prepared for the devil and his angels. For I was hungry and you never gave me food; I was thirsty and you never gave me anything to drink'" (Matthew 25:41-42).

Clearly, a generous heart is not an option for a follower of Christ, yet we all come up short to some extent. If we pray for a bigger heart and try to see Christ in others, our generosity will grow proportionately.

My generosity begins with my relationship with God. I give him the best part of my day in prayer and study.

I support the Church financially. I give to the point of sacrifice.

I realize that my time is my most precious possession and that my willingness to give my time is sometimes more effective than a generous financial contribution.

Taking the time to listen to a friend or colleague who needs to talk can be a great act of charity and generosity. I try to focus on the needs of my friends.

In considering our Lord's teachings, I ponder these words of the Apostle James: "Faith is like that: if good works do not go with it, it is quite dead" (2:17). What do my good works say about my faith?

Considerations for Growth
in the Virtue of **Generosity**

I teach my children to be generous by my example. I try to involve them, if possible, when giving my time.

I try to remember that my greatest act of generosity may be to take time to be with my wife when I am preoccupied with my work or other matters.

I recognize that I can't provide material help to most people in need. But I can usually do something, even if it's something small. And I do pray for those having a rough time in some way.

I reevaluate my ability to give alms as my circumstances change. I make sure my almsgiving does not lag behind my capacity to give.

Chapter **Twenty**

ORDER

And so, my dear brothers, by all
means be ambitious to prophesy,
do not suppress the gift of tongues,
but let everything be done with
propriety and in order.

1 Corinthians 14:39-40

The virtue of the soul

does not consist in flying

high, but in walking orderly.

Montaigne
Essays

Order

Order may or may not be a virtue in the strict sense of the term. But it is certainly a characteristic of a virtuous person. Striving to live an orderly life will give us more time, time for our families and time for prayer. The added time and order in our lives will allow us to take the time to listen; to visit a friend; to go on that outing with the family.

Order leads us to put persons, things, and activities into their proper places in relation to one another. Orderliness generally leads to greater efficiency. It facilitates a higher quality of work. Indeed, as we become more orderly, we become more and more God-like.

One of the more awe-inspiring aspects of creation is the incredible order with which the world functions. We need only consider the operations of the human body or the ecosystem of our planet to appreciate the precise order that characterizes God's work.

A life of order relates not only to the order of things — that our tools and belongings are put in their proper places — but that our activities are also well ordered. We must establish well-reasoned priorities. Our life must have balance with a recognition that some activities are more important than others.

A Christian father has many aspects to his life — spiritual, family, work, social, and personal. All of these are important, but a person living in an orderly manner evaluates and reevaluates whether or not he is shortchanging some area of his life. The most vulnerable aspects seem to be our spiritual and family lives.

I make an effort to keep my workplace neat. Rather than allow papers and other items to accumulate, I file them or dispose of them promptly.

I try to arrive at meetings and other functions on time, keeping in mind that my tardiness can be disruptive and waste my colleagues' time.

I plan ahead and anticipate what needs to be done so that I don't waste time or make unnecessary trips running errands.

I consider potential imbalances in my life. Is my spiritual life getting enough attention? Am I spending enough time with my family? I consult with a trusted friend or adviser to get an objective opinion.

I pray every day and read from Scripture and some spiritual book, recognizing that this is crucial to my spiritual growth.

I make sure that each member of my family takes some responsibility for maintaining the order and upkeep of our household. Everyone has to pull his or her weight.

I try not to collect worthless "treasures" that just gather dust in closets or drawers. I make an objective assessment as to whether or not something is truly worth saving.

I see my efforts to become more orderly as another path toward holiness. Chaos and clutter could never be characteristics that are pleasing to God.

Conclusion

Having read these pages, fathers may be struck by a stark reality — we are both weak and deficient. Yet, we love our families deeply. Recognition of these truths is the first step in our quest for virtue. However, this recognition must lead to a response. And the response must be a concrete plan of attack. It must be a plan that we are prepared to implement for the rest of our lives. If we are serious about carrying out our plan, its components must be written down. Otherwise, it will never be carried out with any consistency.

Remember, our struggle to grow in virtue is — never forget it — warfare. And to wage this war we must utilize all the resources at our disposal — Mass, frequent confession, daily prayer, Sacred Scripture, spiritual reading, examination of conscience. Indeed, we must avail ourselves of all the means employed by Christians throughout the centuries. And, of course, it would be foolhardy not to rely on the intercession of that model of virtue, our Blessed Mother.

We must keep in mind that we can grow in virtue. We grow in virtue through prayer and practice. When we examine our conscience we can identify the virtue most in need of improvement and focus on that virtue each day. If we ask God in our daily prayer for the grace to improve and try to live that virtue in specific ways, we can make great progress over time. And by examining our conscience every day, we make ourselves accountable for our progress. And, I repeat once more that we can approach this challenge with great confidence. God chose us to cooperate with him in raising our children. He will give us the grace we need to succeed if we rely more on him than on our own meager resources.

If virtuous parents produce virtuous children, then, as fathers, we must be willing to change. This is not the time for a halfhearted effort. There is too much at stake. Our efforts can make a profound impact on the lives of our children. Indeed, we must be convinced that, individually, we can make a difference in the world. Many souls depend on how we respond.

Our Sunday Visitor...
Your Source for Discovering the Riches of the Catholic Faith

Our Sunday Visitor has an extensive line of materials for young children, teens, and adults. Our books, Bibles, booklets, CD-ROMs, audios, and videos are available in bookstores worldwide.

To receive a FREE full-line catalog or for more information, call **Our Sunday Visitor** at **1-800-348-2440**. Or write, **Our Sunday Visitor** / 200 Noll Plaza / Huntington, IN 46750.

Please send me: __ A catalog
Please send me materials on:
    __ Apologetics and catechetics   __ Reference works
    __ Prayer books   __ Heritage and the saints
    __ The family   __ The parish

Name_____
Address_____Apt._____
City_____State___Zip_____
Telephone (   )_____
                                  A93BBABP

Please send a friend: __ A catalog
Please send a friend materials on:
    __ Apologetics and catechetics   __ Reference works
    __ Prayer books   __ Heritage and the saints
    __ The family   __ The parish

Name_____
Address_____Apt._____
City_____State___Zip_____
Telephone (   )_____
                                  A93BBABP

Our Sunday Visitor
200 Noll Plaza
Huntington, IN 46750
1-800-348-2440
osvbooks@osv.com

Your Source for Discovering the Riches of the Catholic Faith